# Know About
# Chanakya

## Know about Chanakya

ALL RIGHTS RESERVED. No part of this book may be reproduced in a retrieval system or transmitted in any form or by any means electronics, mechanical, photocopying, recording and or without permission of the publisher.

Published by

MAPLE PRESS PRIVATE LIMITED
office: A-63, Sector 58, Noida 201301, U.P., India
phone: +91 120 455 3581, 455 3583
email: info@maplepress.co.in
website: www.maplepress.co.in

Reprinted in 2019

ISBN: 978-93-50334-44-7

# Contents

Preface ............................................................................. 4
1. Chanakya - An Overview ........................................... 6
2. Early Life and Education ......................................... 10
3. Taxila University ..................................................... 13
4. Life in Taxila University ......................................... 16
5. In Patliputra ............................................................ 28
6. Chandragupta .......................................................... 22
7. The Greeks ............................................................... 26
8. Ultimate Reprisal ..................................................... 28
9. The Visionary .......................................................... 32
10. Arthashastra .......................................................... 35
11. Arthashastra - On Kings ....................................... 38
12. Arthashastra - On Finances .................................. 42
13. Arthashastra - On Mines ...................................... 44
14. Arthashastra - On Gems ....................................... 47
15. Arthashastra - On Other Minerals ....................... 50
16. Arthashastra - On Coins and Metals .................... 54
17. Nitishastra ............................................................. 57
18. Nitishastra - On Virtues ....................................... 61
19. Nitishastra - On Religion ..................................... 64
20. His Ideologies ....................................................... 67
21. Chanakya's Nitishastra - I .................................... 71
22. Chanakya's Nitishastra - II ................................... 74
23. Chanakya's Nitishastra - III .................................. 78
24. Chanakya's Nitishastra - IV .................................. 81

# Preface

Authoritarian rule via a rigid caste system has been the norm in Indian History since the writing of the Vedas (1500-1000 BCE). The ideas of harsh totalitarian rule from the *Arthashastra* played a key role in bringing several kingdoms together in the South Asian sub-continent into what became the Mauryan Empire (322-185 BCE).

Chanakya, the great Indian teacher, philosopher, economist, jurist and royal advisor, perhaps is the only personality who has been accepted and revered as a genius both by Indian and Western scholars. He is a historical milestone in the making of India amidst tremendous upheavals and myriads of reversals. Celebrated as a shrewd statesman and a ruthless administrator, he comes across as the greatest of diplomats of the world.

His foresight and wide knowledge coupled with politics of expediency founded the mighty Mauryan Empire in India. He was a great laureate of economics with a glittering intellect to perceive the intricate dynamics of the various economic activities and principles.

Chanakya envisioned India as one nation. He looked at the country like a person surrounded by problems.

He worked at the total annihilation of problems by the roots. His two epic written creations *Arthashastra* and *Nitishastra* played a vital role in achieving his mission.

This book briefly runs you through the life of Chanakya, his contributions on various political, economical and religious aspects of the country and its people.

# CHAPTER 1
# Chanakya - An Overview

Chanakya, is perhaps, one of those great men who shaped time through his vision and exemplary actions and was accepted and revered as a genius, both by Indian and Western scholars. He is a historical landmark in the making of India amidst the chaos and anarchy that reigned supreme in those times.

Even today he is considered as one of the shrewdest statesman and a ruthless administrator across the world. He had a strong penchant for democratic values. And for this he was audacious even when putting his views through to his superiors. Although, he lived around the third century BC, his ideas and principles show consensus and validity even in the present day world. He was politics personified. Diplomacy in a politically charged environment shows his self-confidence and the ability to stay calm even in trying situations.

His foresight and wide knowledge, coupled with his pragmatic politics, aided in founding the mighty Mauryan Empire in India. He was a great laureate of economics with a glittering intellect to perceive the complex dynamics of the various economic activities and principles.

Even today, one of his maxims on taxation is very much alive and calls for adherence by the governments of the world. According to Chanakya, "Taxation should not be a painful process for the people. There should be leniency and caution while deciding the tax structure. Ideally, governments should collect taxes like a honeybee, which sucks just the right amount of honey from the flower so that both can survive. Taxes should be collected in small and not in large proportions."

Chanakya, apart from being a man of wisdom and unfailing strategies, propounded Nitishastra, the ideal way of living for every individual of the society. Niti is variously translated as "the science of morality", "common sense", "expediency" or "ethics". Hence Chanakya's Niti-shastra contains sagacious wisdom that may be applied in our daily affairs of life with profit. He looked at the country like a person surrounded by problems. He worked at the total annihilation of problems by the roots. Most of his views were so farsighted that they appeared to be prophesies. His contribution to foreign policy is relevant even today. Universities, now-a-days, teach his infallible principles to aspiring foreign policy experts. Chanakya's art of diplomacy is well known across India and practiced in the areas of defence, strategy formation and foreign relations.

As a person, Chanakya has been described variously, as a saint, as a 'ruthless administrator', as the 'king maker', a devoted nationalist, a selfless ascetic and a person devoid of all morals. He created controversy by saying, "The ends justify the means" and the ruler should use any means to attain his goals and his actions required no moral sanctions. All his written works namely, *Arthashastra, Nitishastra* and *Chanakyaniti* were unique because of their rational approach and blatant advocacy of real politic. His views were dimensionally novel. He recommended even espionage and the liberal use of provocative agents as machineries of the state. In politics, he even attested the use of false accusations and killings by a king's secret agent without any thoughts to morals or ethics. The observance of morals and ethics was secondary to the interests of the ruler.

This great statesman and philosopher have been often compared to Machiavelli, Aristotle and Plato, exemplifying his potentiality and influential status.

# CHAPTER 2
# Early Life and Education

Chanakya was born to an ancient teacher called Rishi Canak. Being the son of a teacher, Chanakya began learning the Vedas at a very early age. The making of Chanakya - the intellect within Chanakya was seen even at such a little age, for, the Vedas;- considered to be the toughest scriptures to study were learned and memorized by Chanakya at his infancy. And interestingly, he was attracted to studies in politics than any other topics available in those days.

As a youth, Chanakya had his education at one of the renowned schools in a city well known in those days as Takshashila (Taxila). Taxila was known as one of the world famous education centres and the meeting ground for some of the greatest scholars known all over the world. Students from different parts of Bharat went there for their education. Even kings sent their sons for education there.

The university was famous by the name 'Taxila' university, named after the city where it was situated. The king and rich people of the region used to donate lavishly for the development of this university. In the religious scriptures also it is mentioned that the king of snakes, Vasuki, chose Taxila as a location for dissemination of knowledge on earth.

Endowed as he was with a sharp intellect, Chanakya learnt all the arts and sciences including the *Arthashastras* of ancient teachers and in due course became a great scholar. So famous was Chanakya in the vicinity of the university that he had many nicknames. Different people called him by various names, such as Vishnugupta, Kautilya and Chanakya. The whole nation was bewildered by the cleverness and wit of this seemingly small boy, who went on to single handedly unify the country with the sheer power of his character. He lived his life in pursuit of his vision of a happy, strong and prosperous *Bharat*.

# CHAPTER 3
# Taxila University

The existence of the University of Taxila, now situated in Pakistan, made India stand apart, way ahead of the European countries, who struggled with ignorance and total information blackout in those days.

During the Dark Ages, Taxila stood as a lighthouse of higher knowledge and pride of India. The university, in those times accommodated more than 10,000 students at a time. The university offered courses spanning a period of more than eight years. The students were admitted after graduating from their own countries. Aspiring students opted for elective subjects going for in depth studies in specialised branches of learning. After graduating from the university, the students were recognised as the best scholars in the sub-continent. It became a cultural heritage as time passed.

About 68 different streams of knowledge were taught and studied in Taxila University. To name few out of wide range of subjects taught by Masters in the University were Science, Philosophy, Ayurveda, Grammar of various languages, Mathematics, Economics, Astrology, Geography, Astronomy, Surgical science, Agricultural sciences, Archery and, Ancient and Modern Sciences. The University also used to conduct researches on various subjects.

Generally, a student entered the University of Taxila at the age of sixteen. The four *Vedas*, archery, hunting, elephant-lore and eighteen arts were taught there.

### Turmoil in Taxila

But, life in Taxila was not to stay like that forever, for a new contingency starred in the eyes of Taxila. Thousands of refugees poured in Taxila as a result of the widespread attacks of the armies of Alexander. These people were not productive for the state, as they did not come to Taxila

to acquire knowledge or in search of jobs. They did not have money or any kind of assets to buy themselves the essential commodities.

To resolve the problem, the rulers of the neighbouring countries and the king of Taxila convened a meeting. The knowledgeable people, who gathered to give their opinions on the problem faced by Taxila, gave out their suggestions. At the end of the meeting, it was decided that the refugees must be given cover under humanitarian grounds. So, in line with the decision taken, a stretch of land outside Taxila was allotted for the refugees. They were allowed to enter Taxila after proving their identity with the sentry. In this way what appeared to be a calamity was appeased without much ado. However, the incident was just a precursor to a series of events, which reverberated across India as a result of the attacks of Alexander.

# CHAPTER 4
# Life in Taxila University

Soon after completing his studies, Chanakya joined Taxila University as a professor. Though he seemed to be only a teacher with no relation with the happenings that were taking place across the country, yet it was not so, as is evident from the successive events.

On the contrary, he actually was able to influence the government in a big way. His students looked at him as an ideal teacher, who inspired and exemplified great knowledge. His students respected him and were ready to fight at any moment at his commands. Two of his students, who have been mentioned at various instances, were Bhadrabhatt and Purushdutt. In the events that unfolded in the life of Chanakya, these two played a vital role in helping him to achieve his mission. It is even said that they acted as spies for Chanakya and collected information about the enemies.

Soon, Chanakya got the information that there was a chance of a foreign invasion in India. Europe's great warrior, Seleucus, was preparing his armies to attack the weakened republics of India and there were grave designs threatening the unity and integrity of the nation. In such a scenario, the ruler of Patliputra, Mahananda, started exploiting the common man of his wealth with an object of defending against the threat of foreign invasion and enriching his own exchequer. He also imposed several new taxes on people. Chanakya was aware of the internal and external threats of the country.

While on the one hand, the rulers of the neighbouring states were looking for the slightest of chance to annex the prosperous regions of the country and on the other hand, foreign invaders started moving towards the country with an aim of plundering it. These thoughts gave Chanakya sleepless nights. He envisioned his country clutched in the chains of slavery because of the internal quarrels and differences.

Finally, he decided to move from Taxila University to Patliputra. No doubt this paved the way for watershed changes in the politics of Patliputra and India as a whole.

# CHAPTER 5
# In Patliputra

Patliputra, (presently known as Patna) has been, historically, a very important city, both politically and strategically. Like Delhi, Patliputra has seen the ups and downs of development and great reversals. The well known Chinese traveller Fa-Xian, who visited the city in 399 BC, described Patliputra as prosperous city endowed with rich natural resources. During the same period another Chinese traveller Huen Tsang described it as a destructed city and a city of rubbles and ruins.

Shishunagvanshi established the city on the southern bank of the Ganges. It was addressed with different names at different times, like Pushpapur, Pushpanagar, Patliputra and Patna.

The city was industrious in producing essential commodities and luxurious goods for the rich. When Chanakya entered the city, it was known for respecting the educated people and the scholars. The intellectuals from across the country were warmly invited for sharing new ideas and suggestions for development of the state. It was virtually the city of fortunes, as it recognised the true talent and rewarded richly for the work done by an individual. No wonder Chanakya decided to start his glorious campaign of initiating his mission to unite the country from Patliputra. But unfortunately, the ruler of Patliputra, Dhanananda was unscrupulous and cruel by nature. He was always dissatisfied with the amount of money he had and was throughout the year busy gathering money without thinking about the consequences. He collected exorbitant taxes from his people and hence was quite unpopular among his subjects.

When Chanakya arrived at Patliputra, there was a change in the way he ran his kingdom. He gave gifts to the poor and was on the way of becoming lenient in administration. He formed a trust or committee to administer his gifts and charities. Scholars and influential people of the society headed the committee. It is said that the President had the powers to make up to ten million gold coins. Chanakya possessed an extraordinary scholarship. The scholars of Patliputra recognised his genius and honoured him. Chanakya became the President of the 'Sungha' (trust).

The work of the Sungha was to administer the king's grants and charities. Therefore, the President of the Sungha had to meet the king often. When the President of the Sungha met the king for the first time, the king felt disgusted at the ugliness of Chanakya and developed contempt towards Chanakya. King also could not tolerate Chanakya's bitter but true words. On the other hand, Chanakya was egoistic.

The king, who was not used to this kind of behaviour, could not tolerate him and ultimately removed Chanakya from the Presidentship.

In response, Chanakya erupted like volcano and told the king: "Your position has made you arrogant. You have removed me from Presidentship for no fault of mine. You think that there is none to question you, whatever injustice you commit and however you behave. You have removed me from my rightful place and I shall also dethrone you."

The King, of course, did not keep quiet hearing such words. He ordered that Chanakya be arrested. Chanakya disguised himself as a sanyasi, (a monk) and fled from the capital.

# CHAPTER 6
# Chandragupta

As Chanakya was scampering through the streets of Patliputra, he was pricked by a thorn, he stumbled and was about to fall but managed to balance himself. But Chanakya had his own style of handling things. He looked at the thorny plant and quickly got into action. Though Chanakya was furious with anger, he never let his anger disorient him. He directed his anger in the right direction. Calmly, he sat down and uprooted the thorny plant from the earth. After successfully uprooting the entire thorny plant, he threw them aside and resumed his journey.

While Chanakya was engrossed in removing the thorny plant from the ground, a young man was closely watching the act of Chanakya. The young man was Chandragupta, who later went on to become the Emperor of the Mauryan Empire. Looking at the determination of Chanakya, he was impressed and wanted to talk to the knowledgeable man.

He went to Chanakya and addressed him respectfully. Chanakya in turn asked him about his family background and the reason for wearing a worried look.

The young man stepped forward with great reverence and said, "Sir, my name is Chandragupta. Yes, you are correct, I am in great trouble, but should I trouble you with my worries?"

Chanakya calmed down the young man and assured that if it were under his capacity he would surely help him.

The young man went on, "I am the grandson of king Sarvarthasiddhi. He had two wives, Sunandadevi and Muradevi. Sunanda got nine sons called the Navanandas. Mura had only one, which was my father. The Nandas tried to kill my father time and again. We were more than hundred brothers. The Nandas, out of jealousy, tried to kill all of us. Somehow, I survived and I am totally disgusted

with my life. I want to take revenge on the Nandas who are ruling over the country presently."

Chanakya who was freshly wounded by the Nandas found a companion to destroy the king. Chanakya was greatly moved by Chandragupta's tale of woe. He vowed to destroy the Nandas and get Chandragupta his rightful place as the king of Patliputra. Chanakya said, "I will get you the kingship, Chandragupta." From that day on, Chanakya and Chandragupta worked in tandem to destroy the corrupt and unscrupulous rule of the Nandas.

Chandragupta's origin is not clearly documented, many written sources give varied facts about his birth, family background etc. Some sources say that his mother Mura did not belong to royal background instead she was from a 'Sudra' class who got married to a Nanda Prince Suryagupta Maurya. Some believe that she was the daughter of the head of Moriya tribe who tamed peacocks. Chandragupta's father Suryagupta Maurya ruled the Kingdom of Piplivana or Pippatavana which was the forest area, who died in a war. After the death of Chandragupta's father, his mother moved to Patliputra along with Chandragupta. Hence, he got the name Chandragupta Maurya later and his royal lineage was known as the Maurya dynasty.

Chandragupta was a born leader. Even as a boy, everybody accepted him as a leader. As a boy, he used to mimic the king's court. His bravery and shrewdness were visible right from childhood.

Later, for seven or eight years, Chandragupta had his education under selected teachers shortlisted by Chanakya himself. The art of warfare and the art of governance were mastered by Chandragupta with equal expertise.

# CHAPTER 7
# The Greeks

Throughout the years that followed, the relationship between Chandragupta and Chanakya bloomed, developing into a strong force for their enemies. Most of the historical events took place right under the eyes of Chanakya and Chandragupta, including the coming of Alexander and the umpteen numbers of invaders who ravaged the sub-continent for decades around India. Chanakya's training to Chandragupta was over by now and

he thought it to be the right occasion to let Chandragupta taste the practical aspect of warfare. Chanakya closely observed the movement and strategies employed by Alexander. He also became aware of the weaknesses of the Indian rulers.

The rustic boy that Chandragupta was, had now matured into a sound military commander. The source of strength for Chandragupta and his army was no doubt the power of mind and the towering personality of Chanakya. In that war of independence for northern India, Chandragupta was the physical instrument, while its brain was Chanakya.

The deterioration of the prowess of Alexander happened because of the weakening of Satraps or the commanding officers. Niccosar, a *Satrap*, was killed even when Alexander was alive. Another formidable Satrap, called Philip, was killed, weakening Alexander like never before. After Alexander's death in Babylon, all his *Satraps* were either killed or dislodged, one by one. Alexander's lieutenants divided his empire among themselves in 321 BC. No realm east of the Indus, Sindhu, was mentioned in that settlement. It meant that the Greeks themselves had accepted that this region had gone out of their rule.

# CHAPTER 8
# Ultimate Reprisal

The duo was now ready for the ultimate reprisal. But, they knew that before defeating the Nandas, they had to employ various strategies. Chanakya first tested the policy of attacking the core of the city. The policy met with defeats again and again. With the change in strategy, Chanakya and Chandragupta began the attack on the borders of the Magadha Empire. Again, there were mistakes. The troops were not stationed in the areas conquered. So, when they marched forward, the people of the conquered areas joined together again and encircled their army.

Chandragupta and Chanakya learnt lessons from these mistakes. They now stationed troops in the conquered regions. So, those enemies would not be able to cause any trouble now. Chanakya, with his cleverness, had earlier won the friendship of king Parvataka (or Porus II). Now Parvataka, his brother Vairochaka and son Malayeketu came with their armies to help them. However, the Nanda king had the support of a big army. The other equally important support was the guidance of his very able minister, Amatya Rakshasa. This minister was very intelligent and was very loyal to the Nanda king. Chanakya knew that getting Amatya out of his way was the only way of defeating King Nanda. Chanakya devised a plan, which involved planting of spies in the enemy camp. In a very short span of time, the weaknesses of the Nandas became visible. Meanwhile, the Nandas and Amatya Rakshasa made plans to counter any attacks by Chanakya.

Though today there are no details available on the war between the Nandas and the Chandragupta - Chanakya

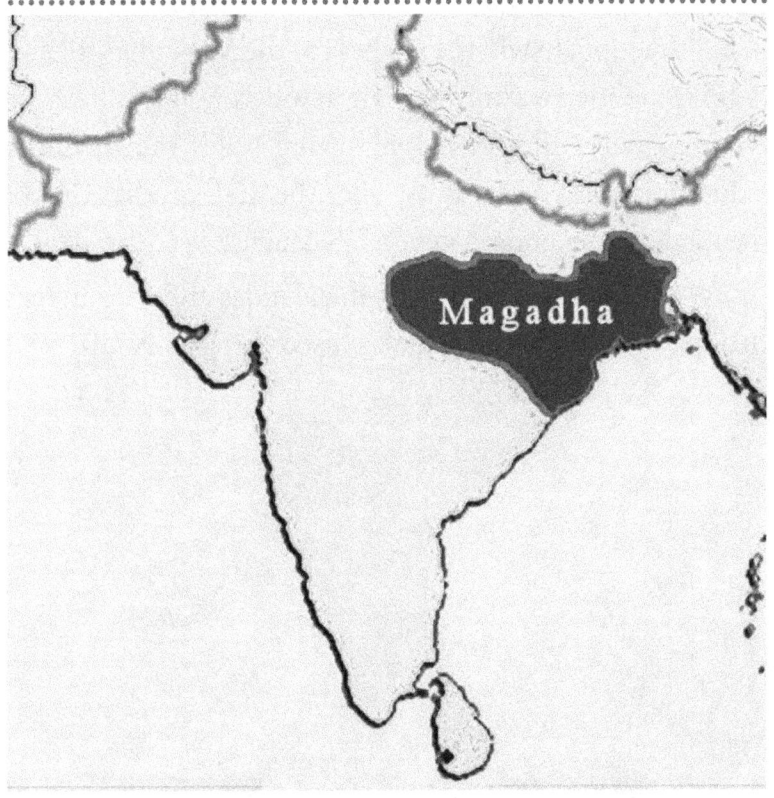

duo, yet there was no doubt that it was a keen and bitter fight. The Nanda king died along with his sons and relatives. Even Amatya Rakshasa was helpless. Chandragupta was victorious proving the foresight of Chanakya regarding his abilities. The old king and his wife retired to the forest. It is said that after sometime Chanakya had the old king and his wife killed, because he thought that if Amatya Rakshasa made them take a son by the rights of adoption, there would be claimants to the throne. He wanted the lineage of the Nandas to be totally eliminated.

After the Nanda downfall, it became easy for Chandragupta to win the support of the Magadha citizens, who responded warmly to their new heroic and handsome young ruler. Kings of neighbouring states rallied under Chandragupta's suzerainty and the last of the Greeks headed by Alexander's general, Seleucus, were defeated.

With the dual obstacles of the Nandas and Alexander's troops out of the way, Chanakya used every political device

and intrigue to unite the greater portion of the Indian subcontinent. Under the Prime Ministership of Chanakya, king Chandragupta Maurya conquered all the lands up to Iran in the Northwest and down to the extremities of Karnataka or Mysore state in the south. It was by his wits alone that this skinny and ill-clad *Brahmana* directed the formation of the greatest Indian empire ever before seen in history (i.e. since the beginning of *Kaliyuga*). Thus, the indigenous *Vedic* culture of the sacred land of Bharata was protected and the spiritual practices of the Hindus went on unhampered.

# CHAPTER 9
# The Visionary

Though the preceding incidents indicate a revengeful saga, yet that was not the whole truth. Personal revenge was not the aim of Chanakya. He wanted that the kingdom should be secure and that the administration should go on smoothly, bringing happiness to the people.

With this vision in mind, Chanakya thought of two ways of ensuring the happiness of the people. Firstly, Amatya Rakshasa was to be made Chandragupta's minister. Secondly, he planned to write a book laying down how a king should conduct himself, how he should protect himself and the kingdom from the enemies, how to ensure law and order and so on.

**Amatya Rakshasa**

To bring Amatya Rakshasa as Chandragupta's minister! Chanakya's thought appears at first sight very strange indeed. Amatya was totally loyal to the Nandas. Would he agree to be Chandragupta's minister?

It appears that even after the death of Nandas, Amatya Rakshasa made several attempts to get Chandragupta killed and Chanakya had to protect Chandragupta with utmost care, until he finally made Amatya Rakshasa agree to be the minister.

Amatya Rakshasa tried in many ways to have Chandragupta killed, but due to the foresightedness of Chanakya he was saved every time. Finally, one day Amatya was caught red-handed, when his men were arrested while *trying* to kill Chandragupta.

On hearing the news, Amatya fled from the country, but could not take his wife and children along with him

and kept them in the custody of his friend Chandanadasa.

Chanakya now gave orders to his soldiers to execute Chandanadasa, but loyal as he was, Amatya returned back to the kingdom when he heard about it.

Chanakya was waiting for this moment. As soon as Amatya offered himself in place of Chandandasa, Chanakya offered him a seat and told him -

"You must agree to be the Prime Minister in the Empire of Chandragupta. You must, day and night, work for the welfare of the realm."

And from that day, Amatya Rakshasa accepted the high post of Prime Minister of the Maurya Empire with a full heart.

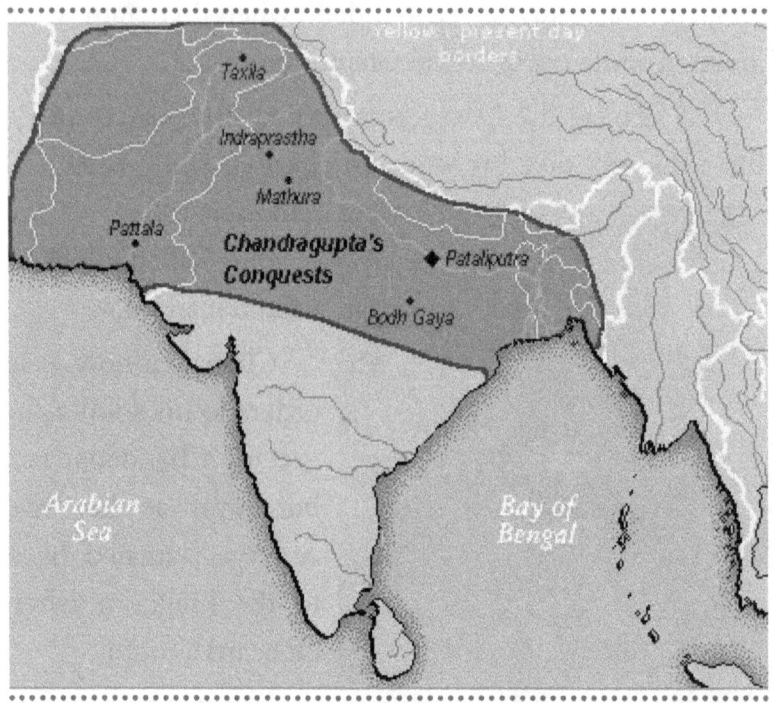

# CHAPTER 10
# Arthashastra

Chanakya wrote the great book Arthashastra. Arthashastra contains detailed information about specific topics that are most relevant for rulers who wish to run an effective government for goodness of the country and its people. Today the book is world famous. Even European politicians, sociologists and economists study this book with interest.

The book, written in Sanskrit, discusses theories and principles of governing a state. The title, *Arthashastra*, which means 'the Science of Material Gain' or 'Science of Polity', does not leave any doubts about its ends.

The *Arthashastra* comprises of 15 books, 150 sections and 180 chapters. The first five books describe internal administration, the next eight foreign relations, the fourteenth and fifteenth, secret practice and the plan of work.

It begins with a narration of how to bring up royal princes and how their education should be. How to choose ambassadors and how to use spies, how to establish safety and security by being ever active. Keep up his personal discipline by receiving lessons in the sciences; and endear himself to the people by bringing them in contact with wealth and doing good to them; many such indispensable aspect required for being an effective and good ruler are then explained. How to protect a king against dangers and risks is also dealt with. Law and order, the duties of the police, how to control the wealthy citizens and motivate them to make gifts for charitable purposes, methods of preventing wars, duties of the astrologer, the priest and others, tricks to be employed to eliminate enemy kings, ways of inducing sleep in human beings and animals, these and numerous other subjects are discussed by Chanakya in the treatise. The wide range and variety of the subjects is in itself surprising.

It has been established that Kautilya's *Arthashastra* records Indians' skill and knowledge of processing gem minerals, metallic ores, metals, alloys and the end products, as well as an aptitude for scientific methodology and the development of an elaborate terminology, during the subcontinent's early historical period.

In fact, Chanakya's Arthashastra is considered to be the first book, which incited nationalism in the Indians and united them for the first time in the Mauryan dynasty. The *Arthashastra* is a brilliant work and is as pertinent today as it was in 312-296 BC, during which time it was inscribed.

# CHAPTER 11
# Arthashastra - On Kings

The Arthashastra can also be considered a treatise on the policy of a successful kingdom. It goes even farther than that, however and describes how the king himself should live his life, how he should choose his aides and how he should manage the finances of the empire.

## THEME OF ARTHASHASTRA

प्रजासुखे सुखं राज्ञः प्रजानां च हिते हितम् ।
नात्मप्रियं हितं राज्ञः प्रजानां तु प्रियं हितम् ।

In the happiness of his subjects lies the king's happiness; in their welfare his welfare. He shall not consider as good only that which pleases him but treat as beneficial to him whatever pleases his subjects.

{1.19.34}

*First, Chanakya describes* in his book how a king should live. The book describes an exhausting schedule in which the king has roughly four and half hours to sleep and the rest of the time is almost entirely involved in running the kingdom. The book suggests a detailed daily schedule for how a ruler should structure his activities. Kautilya believes that it is in the king's best interest to employ agents to espy the government agents of the empire and the citizens of both his and the surrounding empires. Kautilya also describes in great detail how the king's capital and fortress should be structured.

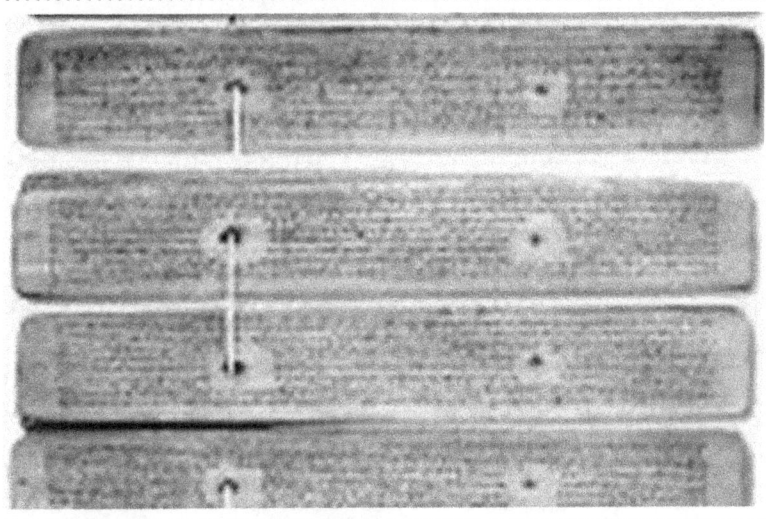

Kautilya writes, "A single wheel can never move the vehicle and be in steady balance. Hence the king shall employ ministers and hear their opinions." In the book, he details the selection process concerning all the public servants, from the ministers (king's advisers) to the treasurer. He insists that they be of high birth, honest and intelligent. Kautilya describes various tests and temptations that his ministers will have to pass in order for their honesty to be ascertained.

The Arthashastra explains the seven components of the state: The king, the ministers, the country (population, geography and natural resources), fortification, treasury, army, and allies. Kautilya goes on to explain each of these individual components and stresses the importance of strengthening these elements in one's kingdom and weakening them in the enemies' states by using spies and secret agent

According to Chanakya, the primary duty of a king is to protect *Dharma* or righteousness in society. 'That king who upholds righteousness and virtue will have happiness in this world and also in the next'. Another significant statement made by Chanakya is that a king who uses his power improperly and unjustly also deserves to be punished.

According to the Arthashastra, the sacred task of a king is to strive for the welfare of his people, incessantly. The administration of the kingdom is his religious duty. His greatest gift would be to treat all as equals. Further, the happiness of the commoners should be the happiness of the king.

Their welfare should be his welfare. A king should never think of his personal interest or welfare, but should try to find joy in the joy of his subjects.

Kautilya, being an Acharya or a revered teacher of King Chandragupta, was directly involved in statecraft, as the king always sought his advice. The authorship of *Arthashastra* in such a capacity assumes great importance. Much before the Europeans could give due credence to earlier literary documents such as the 'Vedas', they recognised the *Arthashastra* as the primary record of objective facts.

# CHAPTER 12
# Arthashastra - On Finances

According to Chanakya's *Arthashastra*, "All undertakings depend on finance. Hence, foremost attention shall be paid to treasury."

Here, *Kautilya* details the duties of the chamberlain or treasurer, the Superintendent of the mint and the Superintendent of the Gold. He describes penalties to be doled out to offenders to the government treasury, in the form of monetary fines. *Kautilya* also describes the values of grains and other commodities. He leaves no form of income unexplored. He also lists the qualities of silver, gold, diamonds and other gems and insists that their quality, purity and authenticity may be assured.

It is interesting to note that *Kautilya* prescribes that the state should carry out most of the businesses, including mining. One is amazed at the breadth of *Kautilya's* knowledge. Though primarily it is a treatise on statecraft, it gives detailed descriptions and instructions on geology, agriculture, animal husbandry, metrology, etc. It is encyclopaedic in its coverage and indicates that all these sciences were quite developed and systematised in India even 2500 years ago. It is surprising that even in the First Millennium BC, they had developed an elaborate terminology for different metals, minerals and alloys. Brass (*arakuta*) was known, so also steel (*vrattu*), bronze (*kamsa*), bell metal (*tala*) was an alloy of copper with arsenic, but tin-copper alloy was known as trapu. A bewildering variety of jewellery was also classified and given distinctive names.

The chapter mentions and discusses the knowledge possessed by the Indians as far back as the 4th century BC, when '*Kautilya*' produced the unparalleled treatise named *Arthashastra*.

# CHAPTER 13
# Arthashastra - On Mines

*Arthashastra* is essentially a book on statecraft. The extensive treatment given to mines, minerals and metals in it proves the concerns of Indians in this regard. For example, *Kautilya* declared that 'mines were the very source from which springs all temporal power for the strength of government and the earth, whose ornament is the treasury, which is acquired by means of the treasury

and the army'. This concept that mines, namely mineral wealth, are a source that forms the basis of finance was always uppermost in his mind. In their survey of the literary evidence in relation to the wealth and knowledge, the scholars rightly refer to *Kautilya's Arthashastra* as a storehouse of information regarding minerals and metals in ancient India of the pre-Christian era.

The chapter begins with the importance of 'mines and metals' in the society and here it is told that one of the most crucial statements in the *Arthashastra* is gold, silver, diamonds, gems, pearls, corals, conch-shells, metals, salt and ores derived from the earth, rocks and liquids were recognised as materials coming under the purview of mines. The metallic ores had to be sent to the respective Metal Works for producing 'twelve kinds of metals and commodities'. Though the authors wish was to show the importance of mines and metals in the society, yet what they point to is their importance for the state and the powers that the state exercised over them. Perhaps, Kautilya himself did not treat the matter so and focused to show its importance for the state alone, as the book *Arthashastra* is on statecraft and not on society.

Chandragupta, on the advice of Kautilya, had amongst its officials a 'Director of the Mines' -the *Akaradhyaksha*. Here, the chapter discusses the Director of the Mines, his qualifications and his duties. The *Arthashastra* advises the Director of Mines to concentrate on the more accessible mines needing less capital investment and yielding large quantities of commodities and large profits over a number of years. Chanakya insists that the temptation for mining highly valuable gems should be controlled, since such materials were rarely obtained in large quantities in one place and the buyers were few and rarely available. Further, it is told that burdensome mines may be leased to individuals, but otherwise all large profitable mines and metal works should be operated by the state itself.

# CHAPTER 14
# Arthashastra - On Gems

Chanakya's *Arthashastra* is a storehouse of knowledge on different subjects.

After mines and minerals, the next section deals with the gem minerals and is treated more extensively than others. One wonders if it is not due to the fact that the gem minerals reflected the richness of Indian kings. Here, the reader is told that *Mani-dhatu* or the gem minerals were characterised in the *Arthashastra* as a 'clear, smooth, lustrous and possessed of sound, cold, hard and of a light colour'. Excellent pearl gems had to be big, round, without a flat surface, lustrous, white, heavy and smooth and perforated at the proper place. There are specific terms for different types of jewellery: *Sirsaka* (for the head, with one pearl in the centre, the rest small and uniform in size), *avaghataka* (a big pearl in the centre with pearls gradually decreasing in size on both sides), indracchanda (necklace of 1008 pearls), *manavaka* (20 pearl string), *ratnavali* (variegated with gold and gems), *apavartaka* (with gold, gems and pearls at intervals), etc. Diamond (*vajra*)

was discovered in India in the pre-Christian era. The *Arthashastra* describes certain types of generic names of minerals, red *saugandhika*, green *vaidurya*, blue *indranila* and colourless *sphatika*. Deep red spinel or spinel ruby, identified with *saugandhika*, actually belongs to a different (spinel) family of minerals. Many other classes of gems could have red colour. The bluish green variety of beryl is known as aquamarine or bhadra and is mentioned in the *Arthashastra* as *uptpalavarnah* (like blue lotus). The *Arthashastra* also mentions several subsidiary types of gems named after their colour, lustre or place of origin. Some of the gems mentioned in the book are *Vimalaka* shining pyrite, white-red *jyotirasaka*, (could be agate and carnelian), *lohitaksa*, black in the centre and red at the fringe (magnetite; and hematite on the fringe), *sasyaka* blue copper sulphate, *ahicchatraka* from Ahicchatra, *suktichurnaka* powdered oyster, *ksiravaka*, milk coloured gem or lasuna and bukta pulaka (with chatoyancy or change in lustre) which could be cat's eye, a variety of chrysoberyl and so on.

At the end, *kacamani* is mentioned, which are the amorphous gems or artificial gems imitated by colouring glass. The technique of *maniraga* or imparting colour to produce artificial gems is specifically mentioned.

# CHAPTER 15
# Arthashastra - On Other Minerals

The *Arthashastra* also mentions the use of several non-gem mineral and materials, such as pigments, mordants, abrasives, materials producing alkali, salts, bitumen charcoal, husk etc. Pigments in use include *anjan*, (antimony sulphide), *manahsil* (red arsenic sulphide) *haritala*, (yellow arsenic sulphide) and *hinguluka* (mercuric sulphide), Kastsa (green iron sulphate) and *sasyaka* (blue copper sulphate). These minerals were used as colouring agents and later as mordants in dyeing clothes. Of great commercial importance were the metallic ores from which useful metals were extracted. The *Arthashastra* did not provide the names of the constituent minerals beyond referring to them as *dhatu* of iron (*Tiksnadhatu*), copper, lead, etc.

*Arthashstra* is in fact the earliest Indian text dealing with the mineralogical characteristics of metallic ores and other mineral-aggregate rocks. It recognises ores in the earth, in rocks, or in liquid form, with excessive colour, heaviness and often, strong smell and taste.

A gold-bearing ore is also described in this book. Similarly, the silver ore, described in the *Arthashastra*, seems to be a complex sulphide ore containing silver (colour of a conch-shell), camphor, *vimalaka* (pyrite) etc. Copper ores were stated to be 'heavy, greasy, tawny (chalcopyrite left exposed to air tarnishes), green (colour of malachite), dark blue with yellowish tint (azurite), pale red or red (native copper). Lead ores were stated to be grayish black, like kakamecaka (this is the colour of galena), yellow like pigeon bile, marked with white lines (quartz or calcite gangue minerals) and smelling like raw flesh (odour of sulphur). Iron ore was known to be greasy stone of pale red colour, or of the colour of the *sinduvara* flower (hematite). After describing the above metallic ores or *dhatus* of specific metals, the *Arthashastra* mentions: 'In that case *vaikrntaka* metal must be iron itself which

used to be produced by the South Indians starting from the magnetite ore.' It is not certain whether vaikrntaka metal was nickel or magnetite based iron.

The *Arthashastra* mentions specific uses of various metals of which gold and silver receive maximum attention. The duties of *suvarna-adhyaksah* the 'Superintendent of Gold', are defined. As per the book, he is supposed to establish industrial outfits and employ *sauvarnikas* or goldsmiths, well versed in the knowledge of not only gold and silver, but also of the alloying elements such as copper and iron and of gems which had to be set in the gold and silver wares. Gold smelting was known as suvarnapaka. Various ornamental alloys could be prepared by mixing variable proportions of iron and copper with gold, silver and sveta tara or white silver which contained gold, silver

and some colouring matter. Two parts of silver and one part of copper constituted *triputaka*. An alloy of equal part of silver and iron was known as vellaka.

Gold plating (tvastrkarma) could be done on or copper. Lead, copper or silver objects coated with a gold leaf (acitakapatra) on one or with a twin leaf fixed with lac etc. Gold, silver or gems were embedded (pinka) in solid or hollow articles by pasting a thick pulp of gold, silver or gem particles and the cementing agents such as lac, vermilion, red lead on the object and then heating.

# CHAPTER 16
# Arthashastra - On Coins and Metals

The *Arthashastra* also describes a system of coinage based on silver and copper The *masaka, half masaka, quarter masaka*, known as the *kakani* and half kakani, copper coins (progressively lower weights), had the same composition, *viz.* one-quarter hardening alloy and the rest copper. The *Arthashastra* specifies that the Director of Metals (*lohadhyakasa*) should establish factories for metals (other than gold and silver), viz. copper, lead, tin, *vaikrntaka, arakuta* or brass, *vratta* (steel), *kamsa*

(bronze), tala (bell-metal) and loha (iron or simply metal) and the corresponding metal-wares. In the Vedic era, copper was known as lohayasa or red metal. Copper was alloyed with arsenic to produce *tala* or bell metal and with trapu or tin to produce bronze. Zinc in India must have started around 400 BC in Taxila. Zawar mines in Rajasthan also give similar evidence. Vaikrntaka has been referred, sometimes, with vrata, which is identified by many scholars including Kangle, as steel. On the top of it, tiksna mentioned as iron, had its ore or *dhatu* and the metal was used as an alloying component. Iron prepared from South Indian magnetite or *vaikrantakadhatu* was wrongly believed to be a different metal.

A bar and a broken sword of steel were found at the bottom of the Khan Baba stone Pillar of Heliodorus (dated before 125 BC). The sword assayed 0.7 % carbon and was certified by Sir Robert Hadfield as having been 'deliberately manufactured as steel' (Archaeological Survey Report, 1913-14, pp. 203-4). This discovery lends credence to the

*Arthashastra* mentioning *vratta* (steel) and various war equipments such as *khadga* (sword). Arrows were iron-tipped. Indian army equipped with iron-tipped arrow and iron swords assisted Xerexes and other Achaemenid emperors in fighting Greece.

# CHAPTER 17
# Nitishastra

Perhaps, the way Chanakya applied his teachings of Nitishastra made him stand out as a significant historical figure. The great Pandit taught that lofty ideals could become a certain reality, if one intelligently works towards achieving his goal in a determined, progressive and practical manner.

According to the Nitishastra, "Truth is the most bitter of all." Chanakya was aware of the realities of life and weaknesses of people. He knew that people know the truth, but still they embrace lies. There have always been conflicts between truth and lie. Chanakya tried to minimize this dispute between truth and lies to a certain extent. The following section deal with a few teachings of the Nitishastra, so that people can know the difference between truth and lies.

- Many things in this world are such that they cannot give happiness unless they are crushed or ground. For example, we do not get colour from Mehendi (kind of leaves) unless they are crushed. Similarly, a woman also will not glow in her true colours unless she works hard.

- A man who often depends on others seldom progresses in life. The moon depends on the sun. Therefore, when the sun shines brightly in the sky, the moon is hidden by its astounding brilliance. Similarly, a man who takes shelter in another's house will always be treated as a lesser being. Therefore, it is necessary to be self-reliant.
- It is said that when misfortunes appear, intelligence deserts a man. However, Chanakya believed that misfortunes are often predetermined and one abandons rational thinking at such a time, which eventually leads him to the ruination
- The teeth of snakes are poisonous. The head of bees and the tails of scorpions contain poison. But the whole body of a man is poisonous. An evil person is the most poisonous. Why does a person with clean mind need to do pilgrimage? How is a man of virtues concerned with

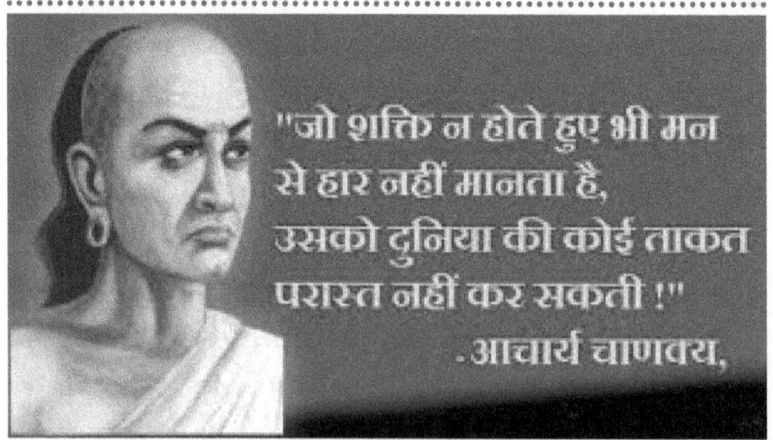

"जो शक्ति न होते हुए भी मन से हार नहीं मानता है, उसको दुनिया की कोई ताकत परास्त नहीं कर सकती !"
-आचार्य चाणक्य.

somebody else's evil deeds? Snakes live in Ketki (the screw pine). Lotus grows in muddy slush. The lotus is honoured only because of its virtues. Similarly, a man shines only because of his virtues.

- Chanakya states that there is a particular time for every work and one who works according to time is great.
- How can an ant ever compare to an elephant? Yet, both co-exist in this world. This makes it very clear that the shape of an animal is not important, only its work is significant.
- Just as Lord Ganesha has a trunk, Lord Shiva wore matted hair and Ashtavakra had a deformed body, yet the world worships them.
- A cow gives milk irrespective of what she eats. From this milk the best of things are made. Similarly, whatever

an intelligent man does, his knowledge is always worth following. By following his talk you will also gain some knowledge.
- Whatever is written in the fate is bound to happen. Only through correct actions and hard work does one get his fruits.
- One cannot lie idle beneath a mango tree and expect a ripe mango to fall into one's hands. Luck will always elude one, who is unwilling to take pains to achieve his goals.
- All birds spend nights on one branch and fly away in the mornings. The world is like a waiting room nobody belongs to anybody.

# CHAPTER 18
# Nitishastra – On Virtues

The Nitishastra of Chanakya also deals with the virtues of life. According to Chanakya, a person is said to be ineffective if he does not possess any virtue. He considers that virtue adds significance to beauty. To substantiate this he added that however beautiful a woman may be, but if she were not virtuous she would be like a barren land, which can never produce crops.

He said that this applies for man too. He may be handsome, healthy and mighty, but if he does not possess any virtue, then he is worthless. Good conduct adds significance to good lineage. If someone of this lineage is without virtue, then his status goes down.

Learning is virtuous. Until a man is successful, there is no advantage from his learning.

The virtue of wealth is in its use. Only that wealth is virtuous, which is put to some use for oneself. If a miser stores up wealth, it turns worthless. Unused wealth becomes meaningless.

However, Chanakya adds that virtue and vice are purely relative terms. They can be determined keeping the time, place and circumstance in mind. What is merit for one may be a flaw for another. One must always conform to one's position in life.

According to his principle, he gave more importance to the knowledge and power of a man. A scholar is always worshipped everywhere. Irrespective of whether the scholar belongs to his own country, people admire him. Knowledge is a powerful asset in his hands and it confers universal adulation upon him. A knowledgeable and learned man can achieve anything.

An illiterate man may belong to an illustrious family and may be wealthy and attractive, but he still cannot gain respect. An ignorant man is like a flower without fragrance. He is a burden on the world. Animals are far better than such people.

He also asks his readers to notice the virtues of great people and not their deeds. Every great man has some weakness or the other. Shri Krishna performed *Rasleela* (dance in which Lord Krishna and milkmaids (*Gopikas*) take part). Arjun dressed up as a woman. King Shantanu was charmed by a fisherwoman. Always remember that no great man is devoid of vices.

Chanakya believed that greatness begins with a vision and ends with a legacy. One should sincerely ignore the vices of men and learn from their virtues.

# CHAPTER 19
# Nitishastra - On Religion

The Nitishastra also includes a whole chapter on religion. According to Chanakya, humanity is the greatest of all religion. Hence, when one looks around and sees different religions, he will realise that humanity is deeply related to religion.

When Chanakya saw human beings entangled in *Dharma*, he imparted the real knowledge of *Dharma* or religion. It is on the basis of this knowledge that people should keep humanity on par with religion, thus improving their lives.

According to Chanakya, if God were the ruler of this world, then, he would have no worries in his life. This stems from the fact that a newborn baby gets milk from the mother's breast.

Chanakya believes that pilgrimage, worship and sacred bath purify the mind.

He also advises that a man should keep silent while taking his meals. Chanakya believes that one who keeps mum while having the meal can get place in heaven for millions of years.

The one who eats fruits and other produce of nature, worships God by remaining away from this world, is a real devotee, a great man and a true Brahmin.

Those who feed the hungry and give alms to Brahmins, get good rewards for it even if they do in small measure. God is always happy with such people. The doors of heaven are always open for them.

A person who does not give charity, does not sing religious hymns (*Bhajans*), does not respect *sadhus* or holy men (Saints), does not undertake pilgrimage, but is greedy and by evil deeds blindly aims to collect wealth and starts thinking too much about himself due to that wealth, such a man must be considered a dead man.

The life of those who do not worship Shri Krishna, do not sing praises of the love of Radha and Krishna, do not read the three stories of Krishna's life, do not go anywhere

> That man who is without religion and mercy should be rejected. A guru without spiritual knowledge should be rejected. The wife with an offensive face should be given up and so should relatives who are without affection
>
> CHANAKYA

to sing devotional songs, are worthless. Their living is as good as not living.

The one who is always enthusiastic in doing religious work, who has a sweet tongue, who believes it is his duty to give charity, who possesses virtues of modesty, seriousness and pure thinking, who honours Brahmins, welcomes guests at home, worships Lord Shiva, all are signs of a great man.

By doing good deeds even a short life span can be considered great. On the other hand, even though a man lives for a hundred years, it will be worthless if he performs evil deeds. His living is as good as non-existent. Lifespan, fate, wealth and death of every human being is determined when he is in the womb of the mother. The time for all these things is decided by God that is termed as destiny. Whatever is written in his fate is bound to occur (Man is a slave of his destiny).

The knowledge of almighty leads away a man from darkness. Knowledge is the brightest of all lights. These destroy the pride. After gaining knowledge, a man is able to remain away from sensory illusions.

# CHAPTER 20
# His Ideologies

Chanakya was a true patriot. Even in those times when the country was ridden in feudalism and was a closed and self-sufficient economy, he dreamt of India as a nation, which would place itself as the forerunner, politically, economically and socially. His magnum opus, *Arthashastra*, depicts in many ways the India of his dreams. When he wrote this volume of epic proportion, the economy based on indigenous ways of production was in a transitional phase, moving towards the advanced aspects of distribution and production. Culture and regional politics directed the way in which trade was done. The main activities of the economy were agriculture, cattle rearing and commerce. Among the three, Chanakya considered agriculture to be the most important constituent of the economy. Covering various topics on administration, politics and economy, it is a book of law and a treatise on running a country, which is relevant even today.

Broadly speaking, Chanakya dreamt of a country reaching the following levels of development in terms of

ideologies and social and economic development,
- A self-sufficient economy that is not dependent on foreign trade.
- A democratic society where there are equal opportunities for all.
- He also supported the development of the annexed colonies. His imperialistic views can be interpreted as the development of natural and manmade resources.
- Chanakya wished that the state kept a strong eye on the equal distribution of land. According to him, the efficient management of land is essential for the development of resources. It is essential that there is no occupation of excess land by the landlords and unauthorised use of land.

- The state should take care of agriculture at all times. Government machinery should be directed towards the implementation of projects aimed at supporting and nurturing the various processes, beginning from sowing of seeds to harvest.
- The nation should envisage to construct forts and cities. These complexes would protect the country from invasions and provide internal security. The cities would act as giant markets increasing the revenue of the state.
- At each point of the entry of goods, a minimal amount of tax should be collected. The state should collect taxes at a bare minimum level, so that there is no chance of tax evasion.
- Laws of the state should be the same for all, irrespective of the person who is involved in the case. Destitute women should be protected by the society because they are the result of social exploitation and the uncouth behaviour of men.
- Security of the citizens at peace time is very important because state is the only saviour of the men and women who get affected only because of the negligence of the state. Antisocial elements should be kept under check along with the spies who may enter the country at any time.
- Chanakya envisioned a society, in which the people are not running behind material pleasures. Control over the

sense organs is essential for success in any endeavour. Spiritual development is essential for the internal strength and character of the individual. Material pleasures and achievements are always secondary to the spiritual development of the society and country at large.

# CHAPTER 21
# Chanakya's Nitishastra - I

1. Humbly bowing down before the almighty Lord Sri Vishnu, the Lord of the three worlds, I recite maxims of the science of political ethics (niti) selected from the various shastras (scriptures).

2. That man who by the study of these maxims from the shastras acquires a knowledge of the most celebrated principles of duty and understands what ought and what ought not to be followed and what is good and what is bad, is most excellent.

3. Therefore with an eye to the public good, I shall speak that which, when understood, will lead to an understanding of things in their proper perspective.

4. Even a pandit comes to grief by giving instruction to a foolish disciple, by maintaining a wicked wife and by excessive familiarity with the miserable.

5. A wicked wife, a false friend, a saucy servant and living in a house with a serpent in it are nothing but death.

6. One should save his money against hard times, save his wife at the sacrifice of his riches, but invariably one

should save his soul even at the sacrifice of his wife and riches.

7. Save your wealth against future calamity. Do not say, "What fear has a rich man of calamity?" When riches begin to forsake one, even the accumulated stock dwindles away.

8. Do not inhabit a country where you are not respected, cannot earn your livelihood, have no friends, or cannot acquire knowledge.

9. Do not stay for a single day where there are not these five persons: a wealthy man, a *brahman* well versed in Vedic lore, a king, a river and a physician.

10. Wise men should never go into a country where there are no means of earning one's livelihood, where the people have no dread of anybody, have no sense of shame, no intelligence, or a charitable disposition.

11. Test a servant while in the discharge of his duty, a relative in difficulty, a friend in adversity and a wife in misfortune.

12. He is a true friend who does not forsake us in time of need, misfortune, famine, or war, in a king's court, or at the crematorium (smashana).

13. He who gives up what is imperishable for that which is perishable, loses that which is imperishable; and doubtlessly loses that which is perishable also.

14. A wise man should marry a virgin of a respectable family even if she is deformed. He should not marry

one of a low-class family, though beautiful. Marriage in a family of equal status is preferable.

15. Do not put your trust in rivers, men who carry weapons, beasts with claws or horns, women and members of a royal family.

16. Even from poison extract nectar, wash and take back gold if it has fallen in filth, receive the highest knowledge (Krishna consciousness) from a low born person; so also a girl possessing virtuous qualities (stri-ratna) even if she be born in a disreputable family.

17. Women have hunger two-fold, shyness four-fold, daring six-fold and lust eight-fold as compared to men.

# CHAPTER 22
# Chanakya's Nitishastra - II

1. Untruthfulness, rashness, guile, stupidity, avarice, uncleanliness and cruelty are a woman's seven natural flaws.
2. To have ability for eating when dishes are ready at hand, to be robust and virile in the company of one's religiously wedded wife and to have a mind for making charity when one is prosperous are the fruits of no ordinary austerities.
3. He whose son is obedient to him, whose wife's conduct is in accordance with his wishes and who is content with his riches, has his heaven here on earth.
4. They alone are sons who are devoted to their father. He is a father who supports his sons. He is a friend in whom we can confide and she only is a wife in whose company the husband feels contented and peaceful.
5. Avoid him who talks sweetly before you, but tries to ruin you behind your back, for he is like a pitcher of poison with milk on top.

6. Do not put your trust in a bad companion nor even trust an ordinary friend, for if he should get angry with you, he may bring all your secrets to light.
7. Do not reveal what you have thought upon doing, but by wise counsel keep it secret, being determined to carry it into execution.
8. Foolishness is indeed painful and verily so is youth, but more painful by far than either is being obliged in another person's house.
9. There does not exist a pearl in every mountain, nor a pearl in the head of every elephant; neither are the *sadhus* to be found everywhere, nor sandal trees in every forest. [**Note:** Only elephants in royal palaces are seen decorated with pearls (precious stones) on their heads].
10. Wise men should always bring up their sons in various moral ways, for children who have knowledge of nitishastra and are well behaved become a glory to their family.
11. Those parents who do not educate their sons are their enemies, for as is a crane among swans, so are ignorant sons in a public assembly.
12. Many a bad habit is developed through over indulgence and many a good one by chastisement therefore beat your son as well as your pupil, never indulge them. ("Spare the rod and spoil the child.")

13. Let not a single day pass without your learning a verse, half a verse, or a fourth of it, or even one letter of it, nor without attending to charity, study and other pious activity.
14. Separation from the wife, disgrace from one's own people, an enemy saved in battle, service to a wicked king, poverty and a mismanaged assembly: these six kinds of evils, if afflicting a person, burn him even without fire.
15. Trees on a riverbank, a woman in another man's house and kings without counsellors go without doubt to swift destruction.
16. A *brahmin's* strength is in his learning, a king's strength is in his army, a *vaishya's* strength is in his wealth and a *shudra's* strength is in his attitude of service.
17. The prostitute has to forsake a man who has no money, the subject - a king that cannot defend him, the birds - a tree that bears no fruit and the guests - a house after they have finished their meals.
18. *Brahmins* quit their patrons after receiving alms from them, scholars leave their teachers after receiving education from them and animals desert a forest that has been burnt down.
19. He who befriends a man whose conduct is vicious, whose vision impure and who is notoriously crooked, is rapidly ruined.

20. Friendship between equals flourish, service under a king is respectable, it is good to be business-minded in public dealings and a handsome lady is safe in her own home.

# CHAPTER 23
# Chanakya's Nitishastra - III

1. In this world, whose family is there without blemish? Who is free from sickness and grief? Who is forever happy?
2. A man's descent may be discerned by his conduct, his country by his pronunciation of language, his friendship by his warmth and glow and his capacity to eat by his body.
3. Give your daughter in marriage to a good family, engage your son in learning, see that your enemy comes to grief and engage your friends in *dharma*. (Krishna consciousness).
4. Of a rascal and a serpent, the serpent is the better of the two, for he strikes only at the time he is destined to kill, while the former at every step.
5. Kings gather round themselves men of good families, for they never forsake them either at the beginning, the middle or the end.

6. At the time of the *pralaya* (universal destruction) the oceans are to exceed their limits and seek to change, but a saintly man never changes.
7. Do not keep company with a fool, for as we can see he is a two-legged beast. Like an unseen thorn, he pierces the heart with his sharp words.
8. Though men be endowed with beauty and youth, and born in noble families, yet without education they are like the *palasa* flower, which is void of sweet fragrance.
9. The beauty of a cuckoo is in its notes, that of a woman in her unalloyed devotion to her husband, that of an ugly person in his scholarship and that of an ascetic in his forgiveness.
10. Give up a member to save a family, a family to save a village, a village to save a country and the country to save yourself.
11. There is no poverty for the industrious. Sin does not attach itself to the person practicing japa (chanting of the holy names of the Lord). Those who are absorbed in *maunam* (silent contemplation of the Lord) have no quarrel with others. They are fearless who remain always alert.
12. What is too heavy for the strong and what place is too distant for those who put forth effort? What country is foreign to a man of true learning? Who can be inimical to one who speaks pleasingly?

13. As a whole forest becomes fragrant by the existence of a single tree with sweet-smelling blossoms in it, so a family becomes famous by the birth of a virtuous son.
14. As a single withered tree, if set aflame, causes a whole forest to burn, so does a rascal son destroy a whole family.
15. As night looks delightful when the moon shines, so is a family gladdened by even one learned and virtuous son.
16. What is the use of having many sons if they cause grief and vexation? It is better to have only one son from whom the whole family can derive support and peacefulness.
17. Fondle a son until he is five years of age and use the stick for another ten years, but when he has attained his sixteenth year treat him as a friend.
18. He who runs away from a fearful calamity, a foreign invasion, a terrible famine and the companionship of wicked men is safe.
19. He who has not acquired one of the following: religious merit (*dharma*), wealth (*arthd*), satisfaction of desires (*kama*), or liberation (*mokshd*) is repeatedly born to die.
20. Lakshmi, the Goddess of wealth, comes of Her own accord where fools are not respected, grain is well stored up and the husband and wife do not quarrel.

# CHAPTER 24
# Chanakya's Nitishastra - IV

1. Offspring, friends and relatives flee from a devotee of the Lord: Yet those who follow him bring merit to their families through their devotion.
2. Fish, tortoises and birds bring up their young by means of sight, attention and touch; so do saintly men afford protection to their associates by the same means.
3. As long as your body is healthy and under control and death is distant, try to save your soul; when death is imminent what can you do?
4. Learning is like a cow of desire. It, like her, yields in all seasons. Like a mother, it feeds you on your journey. Therefore, learning is a hidden treasure.
5. A single son endowed with good qualities is far better than a hundred devoid of them. For the moon, though one, dispels the darkness, which the stars, though numerous, cannot.

6. A stillborn son is superior to a foolish son endowed with a long life. The first causes grief but for a moment, while the latter like a blazing fire consumes his parents in grief for life.
7. Residing in a small village devoid of proper living facilities, serving a person born of a low family, unwholesome food, a frowning wife, a foolish son and a widowed daughter burn the body without fire.
8. What good is a cow that neither gives milk nor conceives? Similarly, what is the value of the birth of a son if he becomes neither learned nor a pure devotee of the Lord?
9. When one is consumed by the sorrows of life, three things give him relief: offspring, a wife and the company of the Lord's devotees.
10. Kings speak for once, men of learning once and the daughter is given in marriage once. All these things happen once and only once.
11. Religious austerities should be practiced alone, study by two and singing by three. A journey should be undertaken by four, agriculture by five and war by many together.
12. She is a true wife who is clean (suci), expert, chaste, pleasing to the husband and truthful.
13. The house of a childless person is a void, all directions are void to one who has no relatives, the heart of a fool is also void, but to a poverty-stricken man all is void.

14. Scriptural lessons not put into practice are poison; a meal is poison to him who suffers from indigestion; a social gathering is poison to a poverty-stricken person; and a young wife is poison to an aged man.

15. That man who is without religion and mercy should be rejected. A guru without spiritual knowledge should be rejected. The wife with an offensive face should be given up and so should relatives who are without affection.

16. Constant travel brings old age upon a man; a horse becomes old by being constantly tied up; lack of sexual contact with her husband brings old age upon a woman; and garments become old through being left in the sun.

17. Consider again and again the following: the right time, the right friends, the right place, the right means of income, the right ways of spending and from whom you derive your power.

18. For the twice born the fire (Agni) is a representative of God. The Supreme Lord resides in the heart of His devotees. Those of average intelligence (*alpa-buddhi* or *kanista-adhikari*) see God only in His *sri-murti*, but those of broad vision see the Supreme Lord everywhere.

www.ingramcontent.com/pod-product-compliance
Lightning Source LLC
LaVergne TN
LVHW091316080426
835510LV00007B/518